SCRAPBOOKING
FOR FUN!

by Laura Purdie Salas

Content Adviser: Melanie Bauer, Manager, Consumer Education & Communication, Fiskars Brands Inc., Madison, Wisconsin
Reading Adviser: Frances J. Bonacci, Ed.D., Reading Specialist, Cambridge, Massachusetts

Compass Point Books ✦ Minneapolis, Minnesota

Compass Point Books
3109 West 50th Street, #115
Minneapolis, MN 55410

Visit Compass Point Books on the Internet at www.compasspointbooks.com
or e-mail your request to custserv@compasspointbooks.com

Photographs ©: Steve Gorton, front cover (left); Gillian Chapman, front cover (right); Keith Chapman, 5 (front left), 17 (right), 21 (front); 25, 26-27, 28–29, 31, 32, 34, 35, 37, 38-39; Cat calendar images copyright The Margaret Sherry Collection Ltd., 5 (front left), 17 (right); Greg Nicholas/iStockphoto, 5 (front right); Lauri Wiberg/iStockphoto, 5 (back); Kaycee Craig/iStockphoto, 6–7; Alinari Archives-Brogi Archive, Florence/TopFoto, 7 (front); Stefan Klein/iStockphoto, 8; Stephen Coburn/BigStockPhoto, 9; Phil Date/BigStockPhoto, 10–11; Duncan Walker/iStockphoto, 11 (right), 43 (left); Rob Geddes/iStockphoto, 12 (top); Sean Locke/iStockphoto, 12 (upper middle), 14, 15; Jon Le-Bon/iStockphoto, 12 (lower middle); Nicolette Neish/iStockphoto, 12 (bottom), 19 (back), 20–21; Rafa Irusta/iStockphoto, 13 (top & lower middle); Rupert Horrox, 13 (upper middle & bottom); Pieter Bregman/iStockphoto, 16–17, 19 (front left); Johanna Goodyear/iStockphoto, 19 (front right); Hansjoerg Richter/iStockphoto, 22; Amanda Rohde/iStockphoto, 23, 38 (left), 43 (right); Kevin Bergen/iStockphoto, 30; Charlotte de la Bédoyère/Search Press, 33; Carmen Martínez Banús/iStockphoto, 36; Wes Thomsen, 40–41; Library of Congress, 42; Phil Sigin/iStockphoto, 44 (left); Jenny Horne/iStockphoto, 44 (right); Greg Nicholas/iStockphoto, 45 (all); Tim Pohl/iStockphoto, 47.

Editors: Lionel Bender and Brenda Haugen
Designer: Bill SMITH STUDIO
Page Production: Ben White and Ashlee Schultz
Photo Researcher: Suzanne O'Farrell and Kim Richardson
Art Director: Jaime Martens
Creative Director: Keith Griffin
Editorial Director: Nick Healy
Managing Editor: Catherine Neitge
Scrapbooking for Fun! was produced for Compass Point Books by Bender Richardson White, UK

Library of Congress Cataloging-in-Publication Data
Salas, Laura Purdie.
  Scrapbooking for fun! / by Laura Purdie Salas.
    p. cm. — (For fun)
  ISBN-13: 978-0-7565-3270-3 (library binding)
  ISBN-10: 0-7565-3270-1 (library binding)
1. Photograph albums. 2. Scrapbooks. I. Title. II. Series.
  TR501.S25 2007
  745.593—dc22   2007004896

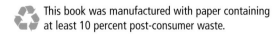 This book was manufactured with paper containing at least 10 percent post-consumer waste.

Table of Contents

Note: In this book, there are two kinds of vocabulary words. Scrapbooking Words to Know are words specific to scrapbooking. They are defined on page 46. Other Words to Know are helpful words that aren't related only to scrapbooking. They are defined on page 47.

It's Your Life

Do you love to look at photographs? If you do, you probably have some pictures lying around. Perhaps you have some snapshots from summer camp or school pictures of you and your friends? Pictures from your soccer games? Arrange your photos in a book, and you have a photo album. But try adding titles, colorful papers, stickers, stamps, and some storytelling. Now you have a scrapbook.

Scrapbooking lets you be creative. You can draw, paint, stamp, or doodle on your pages. You can pick colors and themes. Scrapbooks make great records of things and people you want to remember. A page about the perfect trip to the skate park with your best friend can help you remember that day forever.

Anyone can scrapbook! You can make your project as simple or as complicated as you like. Using your scrapbooking skills, you can also make bookmarks and decorate tins. We'll show you everything you need to get started.

Gift Ideas

Scrapbooking projects make great gifts. For a holiday or birthday present, consider making a miniscrapbook for someone you care about.

Handmade Covers

As well as decorating the pages of your scrapbooks, you can also embellish the covers. Stick on ribbons or pieces of paper.

What Matters Most

Gathering thoughts and pictures into books started in the 1300s, when people in Europe made simple books. They copied their favorite poems or sayings into these blank books. Settlers brought the custom to America in the 1700s. They began adding other material. By the early 1800s, Americans put calling cards, awards for religious or school work, and postcards into their books. Photography became common in the late 1800s. Then scrapbooks began to focus on photos.

Modern scrapbooking started in 1980. That year, a Utah woman named Marielen Christensen displayed 50 scrapbooks. The books showed her family history. People saw these scrapbooks and wanted to make similar ones.

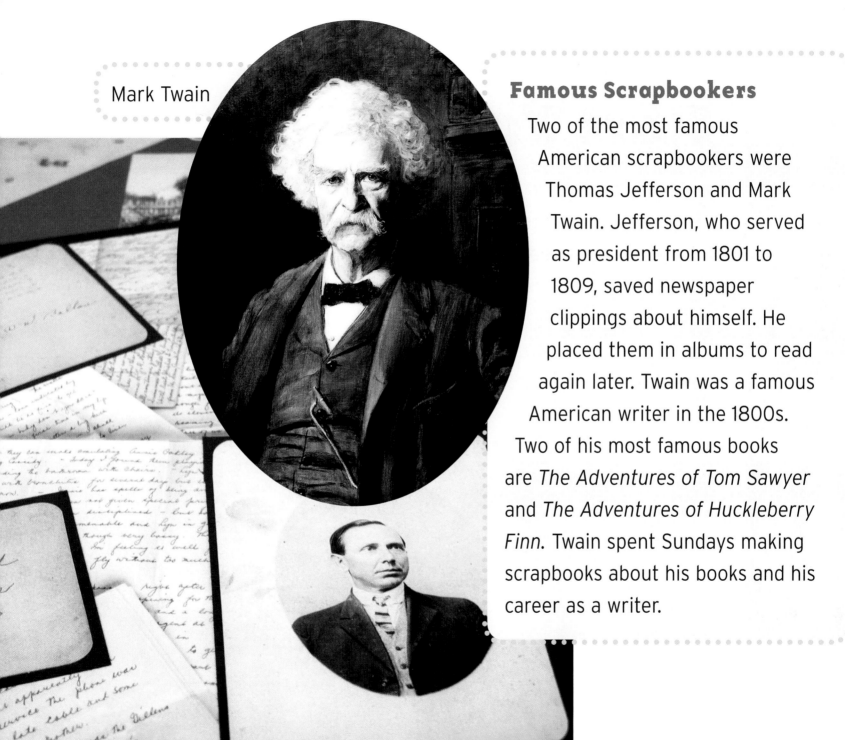

Mark Twain

Famous Scrapbookers

Two of the most famous American scrapbookers were Thomas Jefferson and Mark Twain. Jefferson, who served as president from 1801 to 1809, saved newspaper clippings about himself. He placed them in albums to read again later. Twain was a famous American writer in the 1800s. Two of his most famous books are *The Adventures of Tom Sawyer* and *The Adventures of Huckleberry Finn*. Twain spent Sundays making scrapbooks about his books and his career as a writer.

Start With a Book

To create a scrapbook, you need ... well, the book! You have lots of choices. Ask yourself: What size photos or pictures am I going to put on the pages? Do I want to be able to move the pages around after I make them? Do I want to be able to add more pages? Here are some of your options.

Ring-binder albums are easy-to-use scrapbooks. Each page has holes punched along one side. Open the rings, add or remove pages, and then close the rings to secure the pages in place.

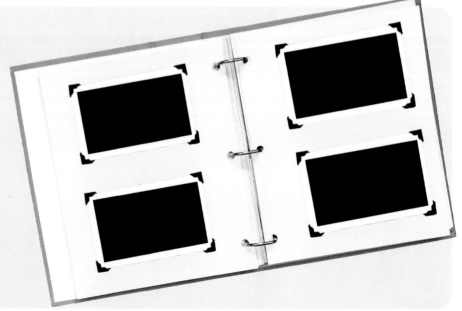

A 12 by 12-inch (30 by 30-centimeter) album is the most common scrapbook size. The large page size gives you lots of room for pictures, writing, and embellishments, too.

Spiral-bound albums look like spiral notebooks. These scrapbooks can be cute and easy to use. But plan out your pages before you start. You can't rearrange or add pages to these albums.

Post- or strap-bound albums are bound by posts or straps, allowing you to move or add pages as you work. To ensure you use them correctly, ask a person at the store to demonstrate. Your refill pages will probably need to be the same brand as the album.

Pocket-style pages are simple and versatile. You slide one picture into each pocket. You can also put writing and stickers on index cards and slide them into pockets, too. Pocket-style pages may be ring-, spiral-, or strap-bound.

Picture This!

Your scrapbook focuses on photographs. Here's a great thing about scrapbooking. You can make a terrific page with just one photo or with lots of photos. Just look at the pictures you have, and create your page based on those.

A single event: Pick out a group of pictures from one event, such as your birthday party or vacation.

A theme: Choose something that you love. For example, gather up all the pictures that show your dog.

Chronological: This means putting your pictures in order by date. Maybe your scrapbook covers one whole year. Start with pictures from January, and then put your pictures in order for the rest of the year up to New Year's Eve.

A Relationship

Maybe you want to focus on other people. That could be your mom or your whole family or your best friends. Gather up pictures that show you having fun with this person or group of people.

Protecting History

Over time, some materials can turn your photos and pages yellow or brown. If possible, use papers, pens, glue, and items made just for scrapbooking. They will be marked "acid-free," "lignin-free," or "archival."

Right Tools for the Job

A variety of tools are available to help you create amazing scrapbook pages.

Scissors: You'll need a pair of scissors or trimmers to trim your photos.

Paper edgers: These are scissors that make patterns as they cut. You may use these to make fancy mats for photos.

Tearing: You can tear paper to give it a rough edge. This can make a unique mat or embellishment.

Punches: Different punches make different shapes, such as circles, flowers, hearts, and stars. The shapes can be used many ways. Try using the shapes to create a fancy border along the edges of your page.

Glue: You can use white glue to add details to your pages, but don't use too much. Wet glue can make paper look bumpy when it dries. A glue stick gives you a little more control to make a thinner layer.

Tape: Double-sided tape is sticky on both sides. It is great for adhering photos to your scrapbook pages.

Paper: You can find paper in an endless variety of colors. Your scrapbook pages can be any color you choose. You also may select different colors of paper to mat your photos. Shapes cut from colored paper make great embellishments, too.

Cut and Trim

After you choose your photos, it's time to cut them up. Really! You'll want to trim lots of your photos.

Before you begin, check with your parent or guardian to make sure it's OK to trim your pictures. Never cut up an original photo, one that can't be replaced. Many pictures today are printed with copies, or they might be digital images that can be reprinted. Those are usually OK to trim.

Trimming a photo is called cropping it. Cropping helps keep the focus on the important part of the picture. If your picture has too much background or it has unnecessary people or objects in it, cropping will help. Be careful not to crop too much. If you crop all of the background and leave in only the people, then the picture won't spark your memories as much.

To crop, use a trimmer instead of scissors, if you can. Trimmers will always give you a nice straight edge, and they're safe and easy to use. You can buy them from craft shops.

Cropping

This photo of a family standing in the front yard has too much detailed background. Also, the family is in the distance. The out-of-focus video camera in the foreground is distracting, and you can't see the people's faces that well.

The photo has been enlarged and then cropped. The family is now featured, and the doorway is no longer distracting.

The photo is cropped one more time. This looks fun, but is not good cropping. You can see all the faces, but there is not enough background to bring back the memory of the place, mood, and weather during the picture-taking session.

Plan Your Page

A little bit of planning helps you make fantastic pages. First, choose and crop the pictures for your page. Arrange them on the page, but don't glue them down. Then select additional papers with coordinating colors or designs. Set these aside. Next, pick a place for the title of your page. Make sure to leave room to write about your pictures. This is called journaling. Feel free to rearrange your pictures (or remove one) to make space for titles and journaling. Finally, think about where you will put embellishments. These are stickers, ribbons, and other items that decorate your page.

Scrapbooking books, magazines, and Web sites have lots of sketches. Choose one you like, and use it as a guide to get you going on your own page.

An Easy Way to Start

Another option is to use themed scrapbook kits. The kits include papers, stickers, and other embellishments. Just add the pictures!

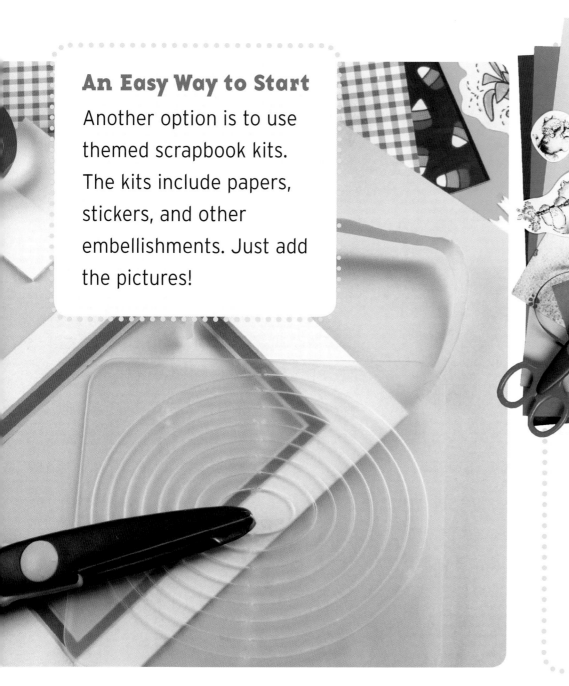

Working It Out

If you have trouble figuring out how to arrange the parts of your page, use sketches to get started.

Frame Your Picture

Most people mat scrapbook pictures. That means you stick each photo on top of a piece of paper a bit bigger than the photo. Then you stick the whole thing onto the page. The mat draws attention to the focus of your scrapbook–the photos. It also frames the picture and makes it look important. And it can tie into the theme of the page. For example, you can use mat paper with a dog-bone print for a page about your dog.

You can buy single pages of scrapbook paper at many craft shops. You can also buy packs of assorted colors and prints. Besides a rainbow of solid colors, papers come in all kinds of prints. You can also use papers from around the house. Notebook paper, construction paper, candy bar wrappers, magazine pages, and other fun items can be used to mat your pictures. Just keep in mind these items might fade over time. Try not to layer them over your pictures at all. If these papers have acid or lignin in them, they might damage your photos.

Choosing Your Mat Color

Can't choose a mat color? Here's one idea. Look at your picture. What's the most important person or thing in it? Now, match your mat color to that item to help draw attention to it.

Stick It

Use glue or tape to stick things together on your scrapbook pages. Double-sided tape is easy to use because it's sticky on both sides. You can also buy glue dots, glue pens, and tape rollers. Acid-free adhesives are best.

Adding Pizzazz!

Now you are ready for embellishments. Use them to add color and texture to your page. Stickers are a common, easy embellishment. Just peel them, and stick them on. Rub-ons look like stickers, but you use a popsicle stick to rub the picture onto your page. Ribbons and fabric flowers add 3-D effects. Just tape or glue them on. Metal charms and brads are common, too. A brad is a metal shape with two prongs coming out the back. You poke the brad through the papers and bend the prongs on the back of the paper to hold the brad in place.

You don't have to buy embellishments. Use ticket stubs from a favorite movie. Add birthday cards from your friends. Stick in travel tickets from a vacation.

Scrapbooking Gadgets

Stores and companies sell all kinds of scrapbooking gadgets. There are punches, which punch shapes in your pictures. There are machines to cut out letters. There are machines that turn any scrap of paper into a sticker. Use these gadgets individually or all together to add variety to your pages.

Computers Do the Work

You can now use a computer to make scrapbooks. For starters, you can print out page titles. And you can type your journaling. You can do both of these in your word-processing program.

If you use a scrapbooking program, you can create your entire page on your computer. You choose the background. You import your images. You type in your title and journaling. Then you print out the entire page in color. Slide the page into a page protector, and place this in your scrapbook.

Photograph It!

Maybe you or your family uses a digital camera to take pictures. If so, you can use a photo-processing program to crop the images. You can also do funky things like tint the pictures different colors.

Title It!

In your word-processing program, open a new document. Type out the title for your page. Now highlight your title, and click on different fonts in the toolbar at the top of the page. The variety of fonts, sizes, and colors are endless. Just look at how different one word can look depending on the choices you make.

SCRAPBOOKING

SCRAPBOOKING

SCRAPBOOKING

SCRAPBOOKING

SCRAPBOOKING

SCRAPBOOKING

A Natural Scrapbook

If you want to create a scrapbook about a certain theme, such as nature, use colors and materials that tie in with that theme.

1. Buy or make a small scrapbook in brown or green. To make your own, cut eight sheets of card stock or heavy paper to the same size. Fold all the pages about 1 inch (2.5 cm) from the left-hand edge.

2. Nature photos have lots of colors and patterns in them, so use solid-color papers to mat your photos.

3. Crop and mat your photos, and decide where to place them on your scrapbook pages. Don't go over the fold.

4. Cut out small rectangles of paper in colors that look nice with your photos. Make them just large enough for you to write a label for each photo.

5. Stick your photos and labels on your pages.

6. If you made your own scrapbook, punch two holes in the narrow fold of your scrapbook pages. Thread raffia or twine through the holes, and tie knots to secure your scrapbook.

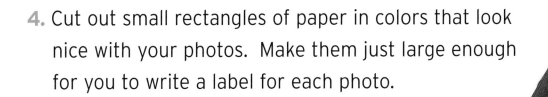

Choose a great photo for the cover of your scrapbook.

A horizontal format is ideal for a nature scrapbook.

Make Pages Pop!

Ribbons, beads, and other 3-D embellishments that stand up off the page add a new layer to your scrapbooking!

1. You can use ribbons on covers or on inside pages. Glue them in position. Place beads on the ends of ribbons. Tie a knot after each bead, so it doesn't slide off.

2. On inside pages, frame a photograph in ribbon; form ribbon stripes on your page; and attach beads or charms to the ends of ribbons.

3. Stick on little pieces of colored felt, if you like.

4. When using 3-D items, be careful that they won't damage the opposite page of your scrapbook. To avoid marks and other damage, it's best to make sure 3-D items won't be directly across from a photograph on the other page.

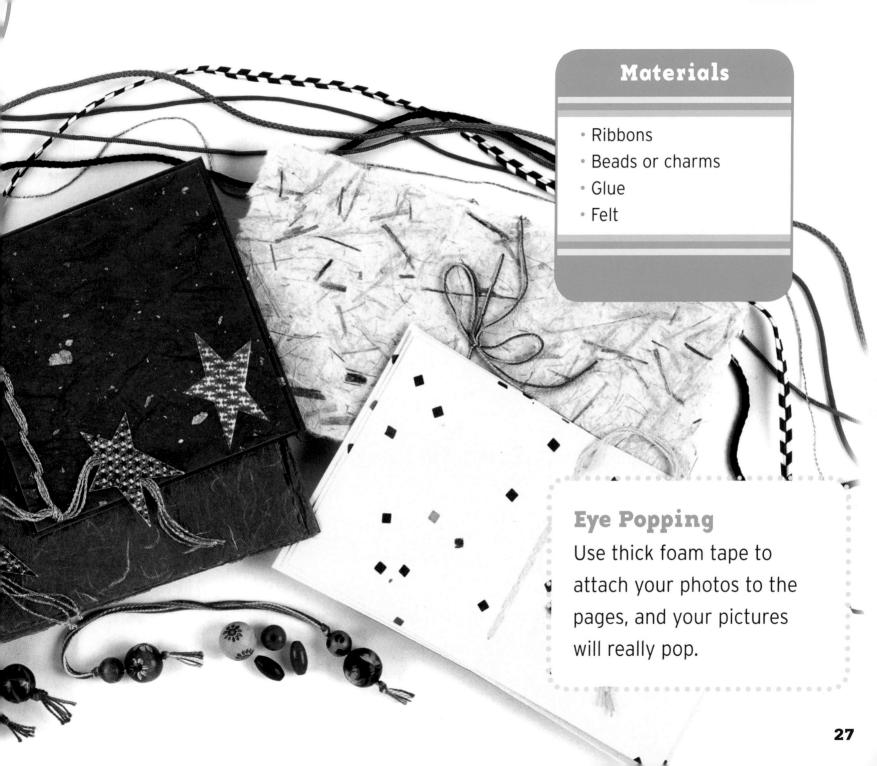

Materials

- Ribbons
- Beads or charms
- Glue
- Felt

Eye Popping

Use thick foam tape to attach your photos to the pages, and your pictures will really pop.

Stick to It!

Using stickers or rub-ons on a scrapbook page is a simple way to add color and art to your project. You can buy stickers and rub-ons that have words or pictures on them. Some are velvety. Others are glittery. Some look fancy, and others are sporty. Go to a craft or scrapbooking shop, and check out your choices.

1. Create your title. You might find a sticker that says exactly what you want, such as "Birthday Party!" Or you can create your title out of alphabet stickers, in which each letter is a separate sticker.

2. Use stickers to play up your theme. If you're creating a scrapbook about football, you might scatter a few footballs and goalposts around your page.

3. Create a border. Place a row of small shaped stickers, such as dots or lines or spirals, close to the edge of your page.

4. Label your pictures. Themed sets that have many words and phrases in them make it easy to label your pictures. They might even replace journaling. For instance, on your page about a camping vacation, you might put stickers that say campfire, nature, roasting marshmallows, ghost stories, and fishing under your pictures.

Sprinkle of Stickers

Don't overwhelm your page with stickers. Keep the focus on your photos. Usually a few stickers on a page is just right to accent the topic or mood.

Materials

- Supplies to create a scrapbook page
- Stickers or rub-ons

Secret Journaling

It's fun to write down the story behind the pictures. That's what you do when you journal on your pages. But sometimes you don't want the whole story right there for everyone to see. Then try secret journaling.

Keeping Secrets

In your secret journaling, tell details about the day. What was funny? Where were you? What don't you want others to know?

1. Pick a fun paper that you like. Cut a square 3 by 3 inches (7.5 by 7.5 cm). Fix the square onto your page, but tape or stick only the sides and bottom, not the top. This will make a pocket.

2. Cut a lined 4 by 6-inch (10 by 15-cm) index card in half to form two strips. You can use plain paper, but the lines are nice for writing on. Punch a hole in the upper left corner of one strip.

3. Write your secret journaling on the strip of index card.

4. Fold the strip into thirds, accordion-style, so that the hole punch is on the front.

5. Thread a ribbon through the punched hole, and knot it.

6. Carefully push a brad through the other end of the ribbon and through your scrapbook page right next to the photo. Then tuck your folded strip of journaling into the pocket.

Purses & Pockets

Purples

Pinks

Materials

- A photo to journal about
- Decorative paper
- Scissors
- Tape or glue
- Index card
- Hole punch
- Pen or pencil
- Ribbon
- Brad

You can make pockets of different shapes and materials, and put the photos inside.

Make Your Mark

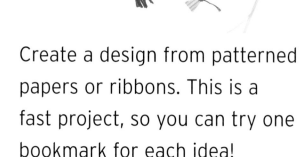

Use your scrapbooking skills to make bookmarks.

1. Cut a piece of card stock into a rectangle 2 by 8 inches (5 by 20 cm).

2. If you want to put a ribbon at the top, punch a hole in the center about ¼ inch (0.6 cm) below the top edge.

3. Now decorate! You can write your name, add stickers, or draw a picture. Use paint pens or markers to doodle a design.

Create a design from patterned papers or ribbons. This is a fast project, so you can try one bookmark for each idea!

4. Cut a piece of ¼-inch (0.6-cm) thick ribbon 8 inches (20 cm) long. Thread it through the hole, and gently knot it just above the top of the bookmark.

Materials

- Card stock
- Scissors and ruler
- Hole punch
- Stickers and other embellishments
- Paint pens or markers
- Ribbons

Extra Ideas

You can also make these bookmarks using thin leather or plastic.

What's Inside?

You can use your scrapbooking skills and supplies to create an altered tin. That means you take a small metal container and turn it into a treasure chest. It might hold your house key or some lip glosses or a pile of collector's cards.

1. Remove all labeling from your tin, and wipe it down with a cleaning wipe or a damp paper towel.

2. Decorate the lid of the tin however you like. Use papers, photos, and stickers.

3. You can layer things over each other. Many people like to cover the entire lid of the tin so that no metal shows. Others like to leave some shiny spots of the tin showing.

4. If you decorate the bottom part of the tin, make sure not to go too close to the upper edge. You might not be able to shut the lid if you do!

5. Things can really rattle around in a tin box. It's nice to cut a piece of felt to put inside the bottom of the tin and inside the top. Glue them down.

6. Paint a thin layer of craft sealant, such as Mod Podge, over the outside of the tin. Let it dry. Paint a second coat, and let it dry.

7. You're finished! Add your treasures to your tin.

Here is another project: Make a little scrapbook to match your tin.

Local Flair

American scrapbooking has spread from the United States to many other countries. And scrapbooking shops around the world mostly sell papers, albums, and embellishments from the United States. Sometimes people in other countries order their supplies online from U.S. sellers.

Still, people in other lands do use local details. They might buy ribbon at their local fabric shop, for instance. And their mementos, such as postcards, greetings cards, and embellishments, show their culture.

A scrapbooker in China, for example, might place lucky red envelopes on a Chinese New Year page. These gift envelopes hold money during this celebration. But a person in Mexico might decorate a page with *papel picado*. This is the Mexican craft of cutting tissue paper into patterns. In Japan, people might use rice paper to mat photos. They will use Japanese alphabet letters and symbols. These embellishments add a personal touch to the scrapbook.

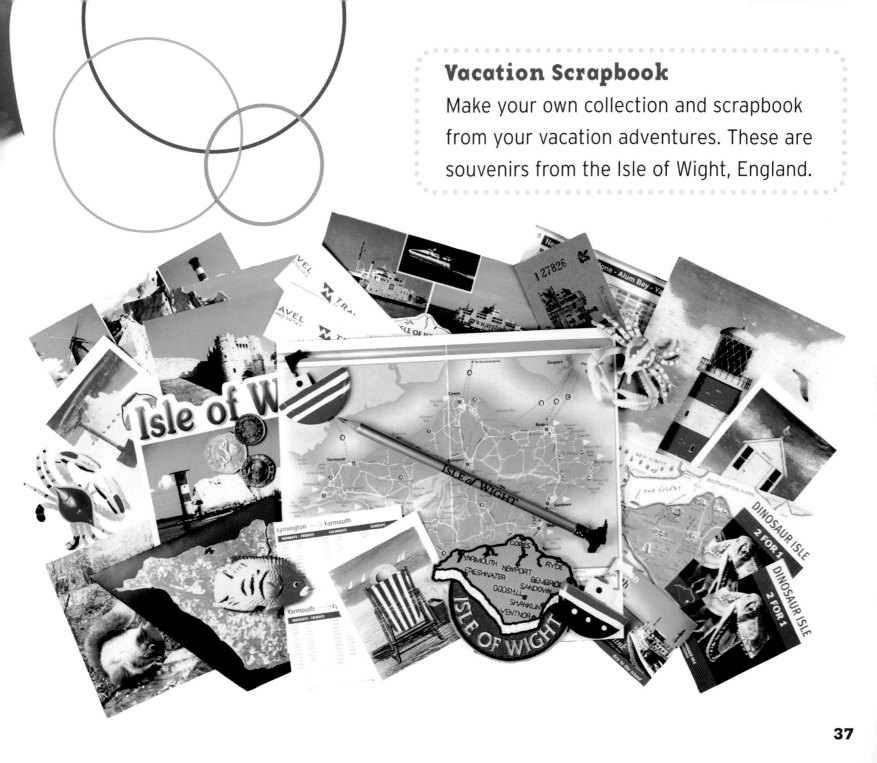

Vacation Scrapbook

Make your own collection and scrapbook from your vacation adventures. These are souvenirs from the Isle of Wight, England.

Where to Learn

There are so many different ways to scrapbook. It can be a very simple craft. Or you can learn many artistic ways to liven up your pages.

Look in scrapbooking magazines for great ideas. There are several monthly magazines. Just one issue will give you enough ideas to keep you busy for a long time!

Another simple (and free) place to get your education is online. Many scrapbooking companies and stores have Web sites.

The Web sites usually have two very helpful features. First, they have articles with lots of pictures and step-by-step directions. Second, they have pictures of completed pages. Many sites have galleries with hundreds of pictures of scrapbook pages. Check them out for some inspiration!

You can also learn scrapbooking skills at your local store. Craft and scrapbooking shops often offer classes and weekly crops (where scrapbookers gather to chat and work on their pages). Perhaps you can even encourage your school to start a scrapbooking group.

How to Get Ideas

There are other ways to learn, too. You can find scrapbook books (like this one) to get you started. Big cities might hold large scrapbooking events where sellers show their products and how to use them. And, of course, it's always great to share ideas with friends.

Two Voices

Heidi Kress creates papers, charms, and other scrapbooking products for her company, Heidi Grace Designs. Kress urges kids to start now! And keep it simple. "I have to say nothing beats good old-fashioned crayons and paper," she says. "I love the feeling I get when I open a box of crayons. It is a flood of creativity for me, the smell of a box of crayons, the wax shavings all over your desk." What's the most surprising thing about her job? "There are no rules!" she says. "With personal creative art you can do whatever you like!"

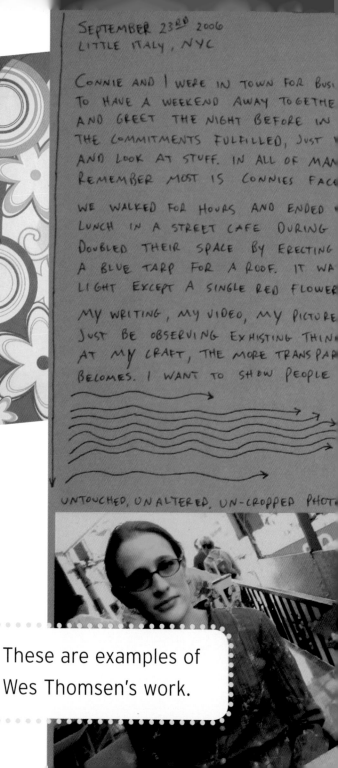

SEPTEMBER 23RD 2006
LITTLE ITALY, NYC

CONNIE AND I WERE IN TOWN FOR BUSI
TO HAVE A WEEKEND AWAY TOGETHE
AND GREET THE NIGHT BEFORE IN
THE COMMITMENTS FULFILLED, JUST
AND LOOK AT STUFF. IN ALL OF MAN
REMEMBER MOST IS CONNIES FACE

WE WALKED FOR HOURS AND ENDED
LUNCH IN A STREET CAFE DURING
DOUBLED THEIR SPACE BY ERECTING
A BLUE TARP FOR A ROOF. IT WA
LIGHT EXCEPT A SINGLE RED FLOWER

MY WRITING, MY VIDEO, MY PICTURE
JUST BE OBSERVING EXHISTING THING
AT MY CRAFT, THE MORE TRANSPAR
BECOMES. I WANT TO SHOW PEOPLE

UNTOUCHED, UNALTERED, UN-CROPPED PHOT

These are examples of Wes Thomsen's work.

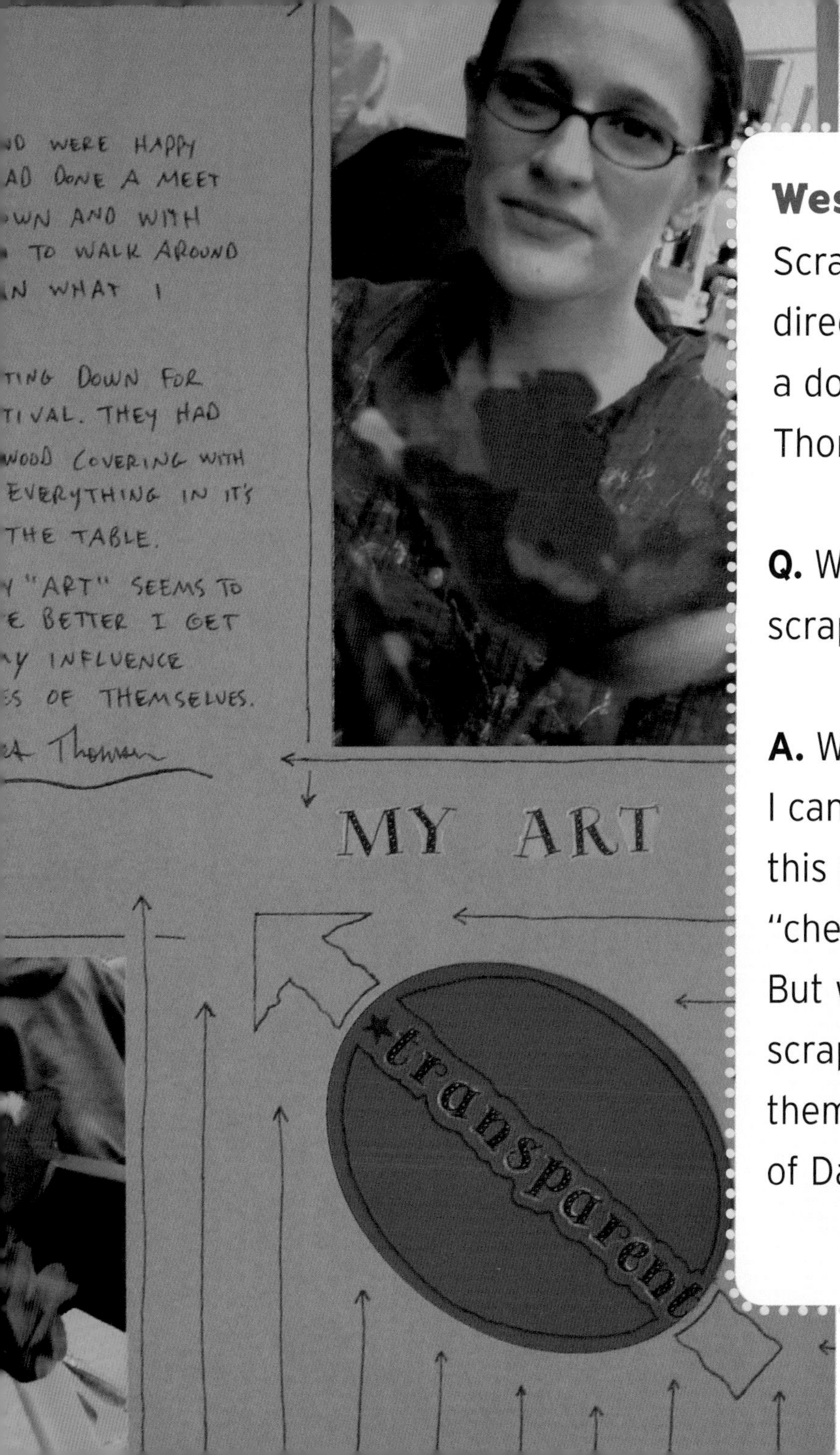

Partial handwritten text (left margin, on scrapbook):

NO WERE HAPPY
AD DONE A MEET
WN AND WITH
TO WALK AROUND
N WHAT I

TING DOWN FOR
TIVAL. THEY HAD
WOOD COVERING WITH
EVERYTHING IN IT'S
THE TABLE.

Y "ART" SEEMS TO
E BETTER I GET
Y INFLUENCE
S OF THEMSELVES.

MY ART

*transparent

Wes Thomsen

Scrapbooking is not just a girl thing! Film director and writer Wes Thomsen even made a documentary movie called *Scrapped!* Here, Thomsen shares a few thoughts.

Q. What's great about scrapbooking?

A. With loose pictures I can say "look at this motorcycle" or "check out this wave." But with a finished scrapbook, I can show them the whole story of Daytona Beach.

Q. Is it OK for boys to scrapbook?

A. For sure! Scrapbooking is just paper and pictures. Guys like us are photographers, writers, and artists. That's what scrapbooking is all about.

What Happened When?

1500   1600   1700   1725   1750   1775   1800   1825

1500s Educated people fill commonplace books with their favorite poems and sayings.

1769 William Granger publishes a history of England with extra pictures in the back. Later editions include blank pages for readers to add their own pictures.

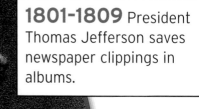

1801-1809 President Thomas Jefferson saves newspaper clippings in albums.

Early 1820s The term "scrapbook" is first used. Scraps are bright pieces of paper left over from printing jobs. People paste them into books.

1839 Photography is invented.

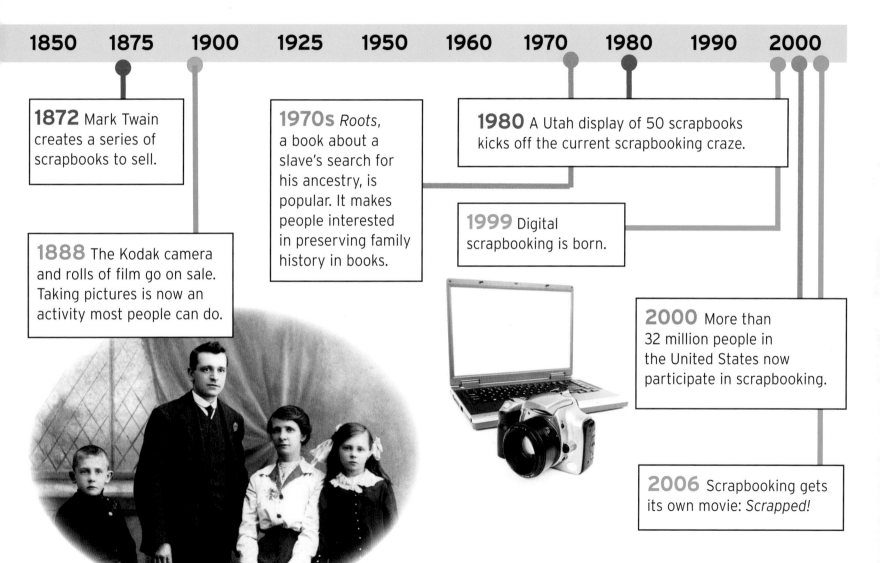

| 1850 | 1875 | 1900 | 1925 | 1950 | 1960 | 1970 | 1980 | 1990 | 2000 |

1872 Mark Twain creates a series of scrapbooks to sell.

1888 The Kodak camera and rolls of film go on sale. Taking pictures is now an activity most people can do.

1970s *Roots*, a book about a slave's search for his ancestry, is popular. It makes people interested in preserving family history in books.

1980 A Utah display of 50 scrapbooks kicks off the current scrapbooking craze.

1999 Digital scrapbooking is born.

2000 More than 32 million people in the United States now participate in scrapbooking.

2006 Scrapbooking gets its own movie: *Scrapped!*

Fun Scrapbooking Facts

In ancient Greece, the philosopher Aristotle and his students used blank books. They put information and ideas about religion, politics, and life on their pages.

Someone is a scrapbooker in almost one out of every four homes in the United States.

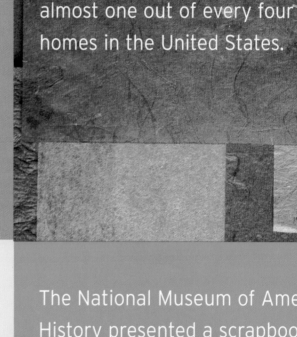

The National Museum of American History presented a scrapbook festival in 2006. At the festival in Washington, D.C., the museum displayed 12 historic scrapbooks.

Kids with illnesses or disabilities do scrapbooking to express their feelings and share their experiences. This is called therapeutic scrapbooking.

One New York museum has a 1916 scrapbook called "Girls I Have Known." Sixteen-year-old Daniel Rochford made this scrapbook about girls he had liked, from kindergarten all the way through high school.

Scrapbooking Words to Know

acid-free: does not contain any acid, which could harm photographs

adhesives: glues or tapes used to stick two things together

album: book with space for you to put pictures

archival: safe to use with your photographs

brad: metal fastener that pokes through layers of paper and then spreads apart in the back to hold the papers together

crop: trim a photo to get rid of extra background. A crop is also an event where scrapbookers gather to chat while they work on their scrapbooks.

digital image: a picture that is stored as a computer file

embellishment: any extra item used to dress up a scrapbook page, such as a sticker or charm

hole punch: simple machine you press on to punch out a hole in your paper or your photo. Hole punches come in all sorts of shapes and designs.

journaling: writing for a scrapbook page that tells the story behind the photos

lignin-free: does not contain any lignin, which makes paper turn yellow and brittle

mat: to place a piece of paper behind a photo, so that the paper frames the image

original photograph: the photo that was developed from the film, or any photo of which that is the only copy

page protector: a clear plastic sleeve that protects your scrapbook pages

rub-on: picture, design, or word that you can rub on to your scrapbook page. It looks a lot like a sticker, except there's no background to it.

sketch: basic design for a page showing where photos, writing, and embellishments will go

theme: subject of a page or scrapbook

title: short name for a scrapbook page

Other Words to Know

calling card: card that usually lists a visitor's name and address, which is presented at a house he or she is visiting

chronological: arranged in order by the time things happened

documentary: movie about real people and events

duplicates: copies

font: style of type (letters, numbers, and other symbols)

galleries: collections of pictures

import: bring an image from one file into another one

online: through a computer system

program: set of directions for a computer to do something

technique: the manner in which something is accomplished

Where To Learn More

AT THE LIBRARY

Hill, Nancy M. *10 · 20 · 30 Minute Scrapbook Pages*. Little Rock, Ark.: Leisure Arts, Inc., 2004.

Hufford, Deborah. *Scrapbooking: Keep Your Memories Special*. Mankato, Minn.: Capstone Press, 2006.

ON THE ROAD

Mark Twain Boyhood Home & Museum
120 North Main
Hannibal, MO 63401
573/221-9010

Museum of Arts & Design
40 W. 53rd St.
New York, NY 10019
212/956-3535

ON THE WEB

For more information on this topic, use FactHound.

1. Go to *www.facthound.com*
2. Type in this book ID: 0756532701
3. Click on the *Fetch It* button.

FactHound will find the best Web sites for you.

INDEX

ABOUT THE AUTHOR
Laura Purdie Salas is a poet, writer, and Web editor. She has written more than 25 books for children. She writes, reads, plays racquetball, and scrapbooks in Minnesota, where she lives with her husband, Randy, her two daughters, Annabelle and Maddie, and one cute guinea pig, Muffin.